MW00630035

IMAGES
of America

LAKE OF THE OZARKS

THE EARLY YEARS

Bagnell Dam nears completion with the lake rising behind it. The date is March 30, 1931. Even this late in the Osage Project, the name of the lake was in question. Some wanted to call it Lake Benton after Missouri's great statesman, Thomas Hart Benton. Others wanted to call it Lake McClurg, after former Missouri governor Joseph McClurg. The dam's builders chose Lake of the Ozarks.

DEDICATION

This book is dedicated to the more than 20,000 men who built Bagnell Dam, and to the men and women who pioneered the business community at the Lake of the Ozarks in the 1930s, '40s, and '50s.

IMAGES
of America

LAKE OF THE OZARKS

THE EARLY YEARS

H. Dwight Weaver

ARCADIA
PUBLISHING

Published by Arcadia Publishing
Charleston, South Carolina

Library of Congress Catalog Card Number: 00102920

For all general information contact Arcadia Publishing at:
Telephone 843-853-2070
Fax 843-853-0044
E-mail sales@arcadiapublishing.com
For customer service and orders:
Toll-Free 1-888-313-2665

Visit us on the Internet at www.arcadiapublishing.com

FACTS ABOUT BAGNELL DAM

PROGRESS

Construction started	Aug. 6 1929
Spillway cofferdam unwatered	May 1 1930
First concrete poured	April 21 1930
Diversion channel opened	July 22 1930
Power station cofferdam unwatered	Aug. 11 1930
Largest day concrete poured	5,080 cu. yds.
Largest poured month	112,980 cu. yds.
Construction completed	April 1931

PRINCIPAL QUANTITIES

Earth excavation	937,000 cu. yds.
Rock	72,500 cu. yds.
Concrete	553,000 cu. yds.
Reinforcing steel	2,300 tons
Structural steel	1,500 tons
Gates, trash racks, guides	2,100 tons
Hydro-electric machinery	1,500 tons
Form work	2,100,000 sq. ft.
Reservoir clearing	26,000 acres

Labor of 20,000 men used in the prep-aratory and construction work which contin-ued day and night.

STREAM FLOW

Drainage area	14,000 sq. mi.
Maximum recorded flow	110,000 cu. ft. sec.
Minimum recorded flow	324 cu. ft. sec.
Average flow	10,500 cu. ft. sec.

RESERVOIR

Area	95 sq. mi.
Length	129 miles
Shoreline	1,300 miles
Water impounded	650 billion gals.

DAM

Length including headworks	2,543 ft.
Length of spillway section	520 ft.
Length of abutment section	1,512 ft.
Length of headworks	511 ft.
Max. height bedrock to highway	148 ft.
Max. width base of spillway	131 ft 10.5 in.
Max. width base of abutment	93 ft. 3 in.
Cost of project over	30 million dollars

LOCATION

136 miles -airline- to	St. Louis
36 miles -airline- to	Jefferson City

75 miles above confluence of Osage and Missouri Rivers.

MISSOURI STATE HIGHWAY COMMISSION

For many years, this sign by the Missouri State Highway Commission stood along U.S. Highway 54 in Lake Ozark at a roadside park near the recently demolished Tower Cave. The sign reflects data accurate before the 1970s. Statistics under Stream Flow have since changed.

CONTENTS

OSAGE Jan. 8. 1931   James Charles Flaherty.

In January 1931, artist James C. Flaherty did a series of sketches of work underway on the Osage Project, which would result in the construction of Bagnell Dam. His sketches were used by Stone & Webster Engineering Corporation, who designed the dam, in advertisements and announcements published in major magazines of the time.

INTRODUCTION

Men of vision began dreaming of harnessing the power of the Osage River more than a century ago. The first were millers who constructed dams across spring branches and the smaller tributaries of the Osage in the 1800s to operate grist mills, woolen mills, and sawmills.

In 1912, a great scheme was conceived by industrialists to dam the Niangua River near Arnhold's Mill a few miles above the Niangua's confluence with the Osage River near "Old" Linn Creek. The proposed dam was to be 130 feet high.

When this scheme did not materialize, the men of vision moved their dreams downstream near the small river town of Bagnell. In 1924, Walter Cravens of Kansas City brought forth a plan to erect a dam here, but it was not until 1929 that plans by others made the dream a reality. The Union Electric Light and Power Company of St. Louis announced they would build a dam across the Osage just above Bagnell at a cost of approximately $30 million. The announcement followed completion of extensive transactions involving the St. Joseph Lead Company and the Missouri Pacific Railroad. The Mississippi River and Bonne Terre Railroad was sold to the Missouri–Illinois Railroad, both owned by the St. Joseph Lead Company. Then the Missouri Pacific acquired a majority stock in the combined railroads. The Union Electric Company purchased a giant steam-power plant from the Land Company at Rivermines, Missouri, and contracted to furnish the company its power needs. To meet this demand for power, the electric company undertook construction of Bagnell Dam, and so it was that Lake of the Ozarks was born on the northern flanks of the Ozarks in south central Missouri in 1931.

The forested landscape of the Osage River basin is hilly, and its bedrock is riddled with caves and springs. Osage Indians were the original inhabitants. Daniel Boone and his son Nathan hunted the land before 1803, and Lieutenant James Wilkerson of the Zebulon Pike expedition explored the territory in 1805. Settlement by people from east of the Mississippi River began in the 1830s.

By 1904 the four counties most impacted by the Lake of the Ozarks had a combined population of more than 57,000, and their lifestyle was based on agriculture, mining, and river commerce.

The creation of Lake of the Ozarks changed both the economy and the culture of the region, thrusting its people into the seasonal environment of a vacation area. The character and friendly nature of the local people is best illustrated by what occurred on May 30, 1931, when the dam was officially opened to traffic. On the following Saturday, 2,914 cars passed over the dam.

"By Saturday night of that Memorial weekend," a newspaper account related, "visitors had flocked to Eldon on their way to the dam and took residents by surprise. By 8 p.m., hotels were full in the city, and 126 people had called for rooms at the James House...[which was] more than could be accommodated.

Hotel managers and personnel of service stations, cafes and other business places called citizens of the city and many took the tourists into their homes overnight, providing breakfast the next morning."

Within just a few years, such efforts to accommodate people were unnecessary as the demand for accommodations and attractions gave the region the inducement for growth and development.

By the early 1940s, it was obvious that a change had taken place. A 1941 account describing the route from Old Bagnell to the dam said, "Between the junction and the Lake of the Ozarks, an increasing number of filling stations, roadside eating places, tourist camps, novelty stands, and brightly painted signs with arrows pointing along winding dirt and graveled roads indicate a widely publicized recreational area."

The 1930s were the years of the Great Depression, followed immediately by the tourist-depleting years of World War II in the 1940s. Despite the hard times, the area grew, and by the end of the 1950s there were more than 260 resorts at the lake.

The pioneer years for the business community at the Lake of the Ozarks were 1932 to 1960, with the most dramatic growth occurring in the 1950s. These are the years largely commemorated in this book, although a peek at even earlier days is also given where appropriate.

It was not easy to chose what areas to feature in this book, because the Lake of the Ozarks region covers such a large geographical area, extending 129 river miles upstream on the Osage with historic old towns on both sides. So a more narrow focus had to be found.

As well, it was not easy to choose the images for the chapters in this book, because so many businesses and attractions seemed worthy of attention and so little space was available. And for many sites, no photographs were available. In the end, those that do appear provide at least a glimpse of what the pioneer years were like at the Lake of the Ozarks and what some of the landmarks were.

Because the construction of Bagnell Dam formed Lake of the Ozarks and made it all possible, the book begins with the dam's construction. Then, beginning with Eldon, the images follow U.S. Highway 54, going west and south through the communities of Bagnell, Lakeside, Lake Ozark, Osage Beach, Linn Creek, and Camdenton to State Highway 5, then north through the Hurricane Deck area to Gravois Mills and Versailles.

There is a side trip to the old town of Tuscumbia on State Highway 52, and to historic Ha Ha Tonka State Park, just west of Camdenton. The book also pays tribute to the area's most famous town—old Linn Creek. It is a lost land that generates curiosity and gives birth to legends. Hopefully, the images and text of this book will satisfy some of that curiosity and preserve the visions of the businessmen and women who first came to the Bagnell Dam area in the 1930s, '40s, and '50s with seemingly impossible dreams.

One

BAGNELL DAM

"Out in the blue hills of the beautiful Ozark country, rich in romance, steeped in legends and brave deeds of its hardy pioneers… the Union Electric Light and Power Company has just completed the building of the colossal Osage hydro-electric element," read a Missouri newspaper account in 1931, the year that Bagnell Dam was completed.

The story of how Bagnell Dam came to be built and how the engineering feat was accomplished has never been fully told, although several publications have told the story in brevity. A brief account of this 70-year-old saga will also be illustrated here, for only one chapter is available to cover the dam's construction. It would take a sizable book to do justice to the full story.

Union Electric Light and Power Company of St. Louis (now AmerenUE), with the dam-building skills of Stone and Webster Engineering Corporation, began the work on August 6, 1929. The lake began to fill February 2, 1931. The roadway over the dam was opened to traffic on May 30, 1931, and commercial operation of the Osage power plant began October 16, 1931.

During the construction, company photographers recorded the history-making project. Much of it was pioneering work, especially the aerial photography. Dan Jarvis, Osage Plant Manager, has kindly made the photographs available for this book. All but just a few of the photographs in Chapter One come from the AmerenUE archives, and those that do not, come from the collections of Bruce F. James and the author.

Bagnell Dam is pictured here with all 12 flood gates open, c. 1950s.

This view in this photograph, dated August 19, 1929, looks west across the Osage River at the site of Bagnell Dam before any construction work had changed the landscape. The valley at this point is one-half mile wide. The great "Osage Project," 4 miles upstream from the town of Bagnell, is about to begin.

A few weeks later, land clearing for the impending dam construction has given the distant hill a crew-cut look and the remaining farm buildings are more exposed. The best farmlands of the Osage River Basin stretched for miles upstream (to the right) of this September 1929 photo. All were destined to be permanently inundated.

This photograph taken in December 1929, is looking west across the dam site from the east hill. An excavation to expose bedrock has been made on the west hillside, which will be the Lake Ozark side. A steam shovel is excavating the flood plain to create a wide ditch that will eventually butt up to the cut on the west slope. The spillway section of the dam will be built in this part of the valley.

This photograph was taken in December 1929, and is looking east from the western hillside. An excavation to expose bedrock has been made in the hillside for the east end of the dam. The cut in the east side is deeper and more vertical. Construction has begun on a cofferdam parallel with the river. Some three-room cottages for employees have been completed along the east ridge, and a water tower has been built. Project infrastructure is taking shape.

The project was divided into three sections—everything related to construction of the dam and generating plant, erection of the electrical transmission lines to the marketplace, and surveys and clearing of the basin. Here in August 1929, basin clearing begins at the east end of the dam site. Before the lake would fill, 26,000 acres in the basin would be cleared of trees and man-made structures.

Once the project began, employees were expected to work regardless of the weather conditions. The work continued in shifts 24 hours a day throughout the project. Signs in the dormitories stated: "If you don't work when the weather is bad, you can't work when the weather is good." Act lazy and you were replaced. The Great Depression was on...thousands of men needed jobs.

This huge trench was dug from the Osage River to the western abutment site. Sheet steel was driven into the earth, and dirt banked along the steel walls. At the river end, a cofferdam kept the water out as the overburden in the trench was removed to bedrock. The section of the dam to be built down this trench would be the western abutment and spillway sections.

By June 1930, work is well underway on the west-end abutment and spillway steelwork and forms. A construction bridge runs down the center of the trench supporting cranes and other equipment. In the foreground, work on cofferdam cells across the Osage River has begun. Fortunately for the dam builders, the Osage River basin endured a minor drought during the construction period. The Osage, notorious for flooding, ran lower than normal.

Bagnell Dam was built during the early years of the Great Depression. Throughout the United States many people were standing in bread lines while the workers at the dam were getting three square meals a day, which were rumored to have been good. This photograph shows a portion of one wing of the mess hall. Each table had settings for eight people.

Men gather at the commissary in November 1929, where an employee could buy whatever essentials he needed for work. The purchasing agent and manager of the commissary relied upon merchants in the towns of Eldon and Bagnell for some supplies and services.

14

The project had both a hospital and first aid station. This first aid station was on the west side of the river while the hospital, which had facilities for doctor, dentist, and surgeon, was on the east side of the river. Accidents and injuries were daily occurrences. A sign on the building reads: "Think of each accident as though it had happened to you."

A small amount of money went a long way in 1930. Rate of pay at the project was 35¢ to about $1 an hour, and even the men who were making 35¢ an hour considered themselves fortunate. The average number of men employed daily was three thousand.

By July 31, 1930, the cofferdam cells were in place across the Osage River. Because the Osage had flooded in the spring of 1929, before construction work began, engineers did not want to risk a flood during construction, so they built the cells high enough to withstand a flood. The cells were driven into bedrock and filled with rock and earth.

In August of 1930, water was pumped out of the area between the cofferdams where the powerhouse would be built. It took six 100-horsepower pumps two days and nights to remove the water and then excavation to bedrock began. The dump truck shown here has conventional wheels on the front and half-tracks on the rear.

16

By October 1930, the abutment section at the west end of the dam was nearly complete. Union Electric invited the attendees of a convention of the American Society of Civil Engineers to the dam site and brought them out from St. Louis by train to the construction area where they were given tours.

The integrity and strength of a concrete gravity dam, like Bagnell Dam, depends upon many factors, including the permeability of the concrete used in its construction. The project maintained a "concrete lab," where concrete mixed for the dam was tested to measure the ease with which water could diffuse through the material. The canisters in the right corner of the photograph contain dated samples from concrete mixed for pours.

The dam was built to generate electrical power, but it also took a great deal of power from temporary electrical generating facilities and mechanized equipment to build it. Materials were brought to the site via conveyor belts and railroad. The construction bridge was used to carry sand, gravel, concrete, forms, and other needs. Train traffic on the site was so heavy the project had to have its own dispatcher.

Nearly 32 million pounds of steel were used for concrete reinforcing, pilings, and other construction needs during the building of Bagnell Dam. Here, workers build forms for concrete at the east end of the dam to key it into the bedrock of the east hillside. A lot of climbing was necessary, and the work was hard and dangerous.

18

The complexity of the project is hard to imagine, until one looks closely at a photo like this one taken in October 1930. The area formed up to the left is the powerhouse section. This view depicts the upstream side of the dam. Some $1.5 million per month was spent during the first eight months, and the total cost ended up at $36 million, a staggering sum of money in 1931.

This photograph, also taken in October 1930, shows work on the downstream side of the dam. The construction bridge now stretches almost the full length of the dam along its lower side. In the background, the Osage River can be seen following the diversion channel under the spillway to emerge from beneath the construction bridge.

This upstream view of the dam structure, taken in early 1931 from the temporary suspension bridge over the north approach highway cut, shows the rectangular intake openings behind the powerhouse section of the dam. It is through these gated intakes that water from the lake is drawn to spin the water wheels which power the generators.

Only one segment of the dam's superstructure remains to be finished, but work on the upstream side of the dam must be finished before it can be closed. Note the path along the hillside (right corner) with wooden railings. A switchback trail was how many laborers got from the construction areas to the dormitories, mess hall, and other facilities on the east ridge.

The footpath is even more visible in this photograph. Imagine having to walk up this long, steep hillside on a seemingly endless, sometimes switchback trail after a hard-day's work at the dam site. The last notch in the dam is being completed, and the date is April 29, 1931.

The reservoir is beginning to fill. At full reservoir, the lake is 660 feet above sea level. The water elevation on this date is 591 feet. The photographer who took this picture at the west end of the dam was standing where the excursion boat docks float today.

The dam's superstructure is essentially complete, but much finishing work at the 511-foot long powerhouse section remains. The lake basin is filling. The dam rises 148 feet from bedrock, and is 2,543 feet long. The spillway contains 12 gates. The 20-foot-wide roadway across the top for U.S. Highway 54 (Business 54 today) is complete. During dam construction, highway traffic used a car ferry to cross the river at Bagnell.

At the powerhouse, work continues as men install the generating equipment. Water enters the dam through the intakes, emerges from the penstock tunnel (upper left corner of photograph), and enters the scroll case (not yet attached) which feeds water to the water wheel (turbine). The turbine will sit in the ring (draft tube) being assembled. Below this is the tube which then discharges the water below the dam.

The water wheel sits in the middle of the scroll case. As water enters the scroll case under pressure created by 90 feet of head on the lake side, the scroll case directs water into openings which feed the water wheel. As water is lost in the case, the case narrows in diameter to maintain water pressure. The water wheel spins at more than 112 revolutions-per-minute. Each unit generates 33,500 horsepower.

The man standing inside of this scroll case for unit three illustrates the beginning size of the scroll case conduit. They are made of plate steel, which was welded together by hand. There are eight units in the dam, and each one connects to a 21,500-kilowatt generator.

On May 29, 1931, the 150-ton crane on the powerhouse deck installed the rotors, which help generate electricity. The dam (Osage Plant) has a capacity of 209 million watts. During the early years of its operation, the Osage Plant supplied one-third to one-fourth of the electrical power needs of the Union Electric Light and Power Company of St. Louis, now AmerenUE.

This is a view of the powerhouse deck and exterior electrical equipment. Metal hoods cover the generator pits. Once water has moved through the water wheels, it is discharged through draft tubes that are located beneath the surface of the Osage River approximately 130 feet below the lake level.

The spillway segment of the dam has 12 floodgates (taintor gates) near its top just beneath the overhead roadway which crosses the dam. Each gate weighs 27 tons and can discharge 101,000 gallons of water per second. Two 70-ton capacity cranes operate the floodgates. When the gates are open, a vernier scale is used to determine the amount of water being discharged.

An inspection walkway that dam employees call "the catwalk," runs the full length of the spillway section. In this photograph, the V-arm of a floodgate is visible. Not visible is the curved vernier scale marked on the concrete wall. This inspection walkway can be seen by visitors and fishermen below the dam. In this picture, taken March 2, 1931, the walkway is not quite complete, lacking handrails.

The dam contains inspection tunnels. This one runs the full length of the dam. This particular view is looking west from the powerhouse and was taken April 29, 1931. One tunnel, called the "unwatering" tunnel, is less than 20 feet above the bedrock base of the dam. Valves in the tunnel are used to remove water from the draft tubes.

Floating log booms were needed on the lake, particularly during the first few decades, to trap floating debris and driftwood to protect the Osage Plant and its equipment. Even though the water intake gates are protected by trash rakes, the booms were still needed. Some were built before the reservoir filled and were laid out across the basin floor. As the water rose, so did the booms.

Traffic began crossing the dam on May 30, 1931. Testing of the electrical generators began in July, and the first load generated August 27 delivered 48,000 kilowatts. In September, it was up to 93,000 kilowatts. The peak load of 130,000 kilowatts was reached before the dam was turned over to Union Electric in October 1931. This aerial view was taken in the summer of 1931.

Over the years the dam has had few problems, but the year 1943 was an exception. The largest flood recorded at Bagnell Dam occurred in May 1943, when unprecedented rainfall almost brought more water downstream than the spillways could accommodate. Debris and trash also created problems and necessitated a call-out of Fort Leonard Wood troops to help maintain a sandbag wall to keep water out of the powerhouse below the dam.

The celebrated north approach to Bagnell Dam passes through a rock cut. Highway rock cuts were uncommon features in the early days of automobile travel. In 1931, U.S. Highway 54 was mostly gravel, south from Jefferson City until travelers encountered this rock cut and they drove onto concrete. The northern approach does not allow for a good view of the dam until you drive down through the rock cut.

People flocked to see the dam even though the Great Depression was in full swing. The dam was in a remote location, roads were poor, and travel accommodations almost non-existent. In 1931, the dam created what was then the largest man-made lake in the nation. To the people of that day and age in the Midwest, the dam and lake were awesome feats of engineering.

The great "Osage Project" transformed the Osage River basin into a vista the local people found almost unbelievable. The lake they had thought impossible lay before them. The coming years would change them also, as the area became a tourist mecca. Some would soon lament the fact that they sold their hill land along with their bottom land, because many would live to see those hillsides become valuable shoreline property.

Union Electric did more than just build a dam and create a lake—they also jump-started the tourism industry by forming the Union Electric Land and Development Company to encourage commercial development. They built the first boat dock at the western end of the dam, established the first excursion boat service, constructed a luxury hotel at the east end, and built some of the first tourist cottages.

This large parking area at the west end of the dam, as it looked 20 years later, was built by Union Electric for vacationers—especially those patronizing the Lakeside Casino restaurant and the Union Electric boat dock where excursion boat rides were available. By 1934, there were 57 privately owned resorts and motels and 84 other businesses west of this point.

It is uncommon to see all of the floodgates at Bagnell Dam wide open, but when it occurs it is a spectacular event. This photograph is from the collection of Bruce F. James, whose late father, William Bruce James, was Osage plant manager for more than 25 years. W. Bruce James began working at the dam as an electrician's helper in 1931 before the dam was complete, and rose through the ranks to become plant manager.

Two

ELDON TO TUSCUMBIA

In 1930, Eldon was transformed from a country town to a bustling little city, due to the construction of Bagnell Dam. It is located at the junction of two major highways, U.S. Highway 54 and State Highway 52. Eldon is about 12 miles north of Bagnell Dam.

Established in 1882, Eldon became a railhead for a branch of the Missouri Pacific Railroad. A spur was soon extended south to the town of "old" Bagnell on the banks of the Osage River.

Before the construction of the dam, Eldon was a farm commodities, cheese, and clothing manufacturing center; however, the coming of the lake allowed Eldon to become a tourist center. After 1931, local advertising promoted tourist camps, hotels, cafes, garages, filling stations, and the local caves.

The junction of Highways 54 and 52, about 3 miles south of Eldon, developed into a crossroads of tourist-oriented businesses which gave the area a distinctive look and a unique combination of attractions.

Tuscumbia, located on Highway 52, 9 miles east of the junction of 54–52 along the banks of the Osage River, is the county seat of Miller County. It dates to 1837, when its post office was established. Tuscumbia's past is strongly identified with steamboat commerce on the Osage River, which ended with the construction of the dam.

The pictures of this interesting area north of Bagnell Dam used in this chapter come from the collections of James E. Lawrence, the Miller County Historical Society, and the author.

Gone and nearly forgotten, because so many who knew him are deceased, is the flamboyant Clarence Musser (short man on left with tie) and the nightlife at Musser's Resort south of Eldon. Some great black jazz bands and orchestras from Kansas City played in the resort's ballroom and entertained local people and tourists in the early 1940s.

Eldon was named and platted by George R. Weeks in 1882. The name "Eldon" comes from the English duke of the same name. Weeks simply thought it sounded good. Streets running east and west were numbered, while streets running north and south were largely named after species of trees. The main business district was along Maple Street, seen here looking south in 1904. The street was paved in 1913.

By the late 1950s, paved and with street lamps in place, Maple Street had a cleaner look. The building on the left, occupied by the Ben Franklin Store, was built in 1905 to house the Becker Brothers store. On the opposite side of the street is a rock-veneered building built in the "giraffe rock" style of architecture so popular in the 1930s and '40s.

The first Missouri Pacific Railroad depot built in Eldon, at the corner of Maple and Second Streets, was destroyed by fire March 17, 1886. A new depot was built in 1888. In this view in front of the second depot, looking north along Maple Street, people are seen boarding a horse-drawn bus. One horse is keeping an eye on the small black dog by the man standing.

In 1904, a much more elegant train depot was constructed in Eldon at a cost of $12,000. R.S. Harvey, who lead the project, was a popular community leader of the day. It became known as the Rock Island Depot. This is a 1909 view of one end of the building, which no longer exists.

Randles Court was one of the first motels built in Eldon along U.S. Highway 54. It began as Loyd A. Boots Cottage Court, and was constructed in the 1930s. Its interesting cobblestone architecture gives it a special distinction. Cobblestone buildings were once common in the Ozarks. Randle's Court is one of the few cobblestone structures left in the lake area.

After the completion of Bagnell Dam, tourist development began at the junction of Highways 54–52 south of Eldon. Musser's Ozark Resort was the first sizable establishment at the junction, and became a popular entertainment center north of the dam. Clarence C. Musser, operator of the establishment, was an excellent promoter. He achieved success but also a good measure of notoriety.

Musser's Resort complex included a gas station, cabins, 14-room hotel, dining room, ballroom, trailer court, tennis court, driving range, and more. The buildings were erected in 1936 by the Musser Tavern Company of Kansas City and designed by Marshall Harrison.

In 1946, Musser shot a man in Eldon, pleaded self defense, and was acquitted. During the trial, the resort was sold to Jeff and Sylvia Mitchell. One year later they sold to James Lawrence, James Hannaford, and Francis Biselx. The new partners promptly changed the name to El Rancho Resort. Today, the entire complex is gone, and only the name El Rancho survives for a new business at the junction.

Tuscumbia is located on the banks of the Osage River about 9 miles east of U.S. Highway 54 on State Highway 52. This 1890 view of Schyler's boat landing shows the ferry (to the left) and steamer *Frederick*. River traffic was big business for Tuscumbia and the whole of Miller County in the late 1800s.

An excursion party boards the steamer *J.R. Wells* at Schyler's ferry landing at Tuscumbia, August 1903. It would be two more years before a bridge would be built across the Osage River at Tuscumbia, replacing the ferry. The *J.R. Wells* moved freight and passengers on the Osage, Missouri, and Mississippi Rivers.

This attractive suspension bridge was built across the Osage River at Tuscumbia in 1905 and dedicated on August 4. It was the first bridge built across the Osage in Miller County and was a toll bridge. It was in service until 1933.

By 1930, the bridge shown in the top photograph was obsolete, and a new bridge was needed at Tuscumbia. Automobiles were not a consideration when the first bridge was built. The new bridge was dedicated in 1933. In this rare old photograph, both bridges can be seen. A close look reveals that while the ends and cables are still in place on the old bridge, most of its floor is missing.

In the late 1800s and early 1900s, Anchor Roller Mills was the most substantial business enterprise in Tuscumbia. In this 1890s view, local farmers are seen hauling wheat to the mill. The first Anchor Roller Mills building was close to the river, but was later relocated to this site by Phillip F. Hauenstein. Before becoming a miller, Hauenstein had been a riverboat captain.

With the advent of the 1950s, roadside attractions sprang up along U.S. Highway 54 south of El Rancho Resort. The Ozark Deer Farm was about a half-mile south of El Rancho. The deer farm had many conventional animals, but also exhibited a few unusual animals such as a live, five-legged ox. The attraction later became known as Animal World, but it no longer exists.

Next door to the Ozark Deer Farm was Max Allen's Reptile Gardens, owned by the Nickerson family of Nickerson Farms fame. The business was managed by their son, Max Allen. The attraction featured more than three hundred varieties of snakes and lizards. The reptile gardens are long gone, and the old rock building has become a ruin, overgrown with ivy on an abandoned section of U.S. Highway 54.

Max Allen is seen here milking a venomous Florida Cottonmouth water moccasin. The venom was sold to medical firms and brought the reptile gardens $100 an ounce. Max achieved quite a measure of fame with his television appearances and animal-gathering safaris to remote corners of the world. Some of the snakes exhibited at Max Allen's Reptile Gardens were among the world's most venomous.

Located almost a mile west of the deer farm and reptile gardens was Stark Caverns. While the deer farm and reptile gardens no longer exist, the cave is still a local attraction. It has had several commercial names and is now called Fantasy World Caverns. In this May 12, 1950 photograph, we see one of the first tour groups to visit the cave.

The gift shop building shown along the right side in the top photograph was eventually relocated across the wide cave entrance. The huge entrance passage and its lofty rooms were used in the 1800s and early 1900s by the local people for many kinds of recreational activities. The area shown here was eventually excavated for an artificial lake.

Three

BAGNELL TO LAKESIDE

The town of Bagnell, often called "Old" Bagnell, is located about 1.5 miles east of Highway 54 on Route V, and 4 miles downstream from Bagnell Dam on the Osage River. It is the town from which Bagnell Dam took its name. The town itself was named for William Bagnell, a railroad contractor.

Bagnell sprang up after a spur of the Missouri Pacific Railroad was built to that point for the railroad tie industry in 1880, which prospered until about 1910. The ties were rafted down the Osage River from the Niangua, Gravois, and Glaize Rivers, which are major tributaries of the upper Osage.

When construction of Bagnell Dam began, the town of Bagnell experienced a boom and briefly became a thriving center of commerce, largely because a spur was built from Bagnell to the dam construction site. Two disastrous fires that nearly destroyed every building in town in 1931, followed by a record-breaking flood in 1943, reduced the town to a fishing hamlet, and it never recovered.

Lakeside, now part of Lake Ozark, is a developed area which surrounds Bagnell Dam. During the construction period it was located mainly on the east side of the river.

The photos of Bagnell and Lakeside used in this chapter come from the collections of the Miller County Historical Society, Camden County Historical Society, Missouri State Archives, AmerenUE, Bruce F. James, and the author.

This rare, late 1929 view of Main Street in Old Bagnell shows the town at the height of its boom during the construction of Bagnell Dam. Virtually all of the buildings shown in this photo were destroyed by fire on March 16, 1931.

Tie rafts were common sights on the Osage River from 1880–1910. Ties were hewn on two sides, were 6 inches deep, 8 feet long, and as wide as possible. Made preferably from white oak, tie hackers would "chute" the ties over river bluffs and down slopes to the river and create rafts made from five to seven hundred ties. They all wound up at Bagnell for shipment to market.

Once called the "Tie Capitol of the World," the Old Bagnell tie yards would sometimes have as many as 30,000 ties in storage awaiting shipment through Eldon. Each tie was branded, and Number One ties brought 20¢. Culls brought 15¢. During its existence, the industry decimated the virgin timber of the Osage River basin.

This 1950s aerial photograph taken by the late Gerald Massie of the Missouri Division of Tourism and Economic Development, shows the west end of Bagnell Dam and its commercial area. The large parking lot area defines the extent of Lakeside at the west end of the dam. Most of this land belonged to Union Electric until the 1940s, when it was sold to private owners.

This late 1950s aerial view of Bagnell Dam taken by Massie shows some of the land at the east and northeast end of the dam which defines Lakeside. The seaplane visible in this photograph is giving tourists a flight over the lake. The plane launched from the west end of the dam at Loc-Wood Dock.

This view of the Oak Lodge facilities, built to house women employees during the construction of Bagnell Dam, was taken in early 1931. The rock wall in the foreground is the upper part of the road cut at the northern approach to the dam. A small suspension bridge crossed the gap during the construction period.

The U.E. Administration Lodge, seen here on August 29, 1930, was nearly complete when this photograph was taken. The 29-room structure was built at a cost of $135,000. Hand-hewn pine logs brought from the state of Washington were used in its construction, and rooms were named after town sites which were inundated by the lake. President Franklin D. Roosevelt is said to have once stayed in one of the bedrooms during a visit.

The wings of the lodge contained bedrooms, bathrooms, and kitchen-dining facilities. The central chamber is a room 78 feet by 54 feet by 35 feet high. This early 1950s photograph by Massie shows the original furnishings. A large window behind the photographer (not visible in the photograph) has a commanding view of the lake and dam.

The view of Lake of the Ozarks from the deck of the lodge is popular. The lodge is on a prominent hill along the north shore of the lake, 1 mile upstream from the dam. In the 1940s, Union Electric sold the facility to Cyrus Willmore, whose name it still bears. Union Electric once again became the owner in the 1990s. The building was restored and is now a museum and information center for the Lake Area Chamber of Commerce.

Among historic structures built by Union Electric that have not survived to the present day is the Lakeside Casino. It stood near the west end of the dam across from the large parking lot seen in a previous photograph. The casino was a delightful place to dance and enjoy high-class fountain service and meals.

Holiday House was owned and operated by the Union Electric Land and Development Company. It stood on the hill east of the dam overlooking the dam and lake. The business catered to an exclusive clientele and had rooms and cottages which would accommodate 52 guests. It was a seasonal operation and usually filled to capacity. Holiday House is no longer standing.

During dam construction, people could view the activities from an observation platform on top of the hill overlooking the dam site. The observation deck can be seen in this 1930 photograph just to the left of the house. A flag flies above the deck. The deck was removed after the dam was completed, but a new one was recently built very close to the original site.

Among the displays on the observation platform in 1930 was this one with models that demonstrated three different functions of the dam. Display panels explained the Osage Project and promoted Union Electric Light and Power Company, as well as Stone and Webster Engineering Corporation, who designed and built the dam. Stone and Webster had constructed several large dams before Bagnell.

During the construction of the dam, Lakeside had its own airport in the valley about 2 miles below the dam. The runways for Sky Lake Airport displaced cornfields, and were, for the most part, crushed limestone. In the background at the base of the distant hillside was the Houston Yard for storing dam construction equipment and supplies. Today these fields are again cultivated, but the airport is gone.

This vintage photo of the Ford Tri-motor airplane used to photo-document the construction of Bagnell Dam, flew regularly from the airport. The plane gave Union Electric and Stone and Webster officials a way to track the progress of their project. Some of the local people had their first airplane ride on this craft and came back to the ground swearing they'd never fly again.

This elaborate boat dock was built by the Union Electric Land and Development Company and was the first dock to be put into service at the west end of Bagnell Dam. Visitors had their choice of several different types of boats for a trip on the lake, including excursion boats and speed boats. The boats were also owned by Union Electric.

Union Electric formed the Union Electric Land and Development Company after the dam was built to encourage commercial development. In the 1940s, the federal government ruled that utility companies could not own any property for which a need could not be justified. The dock in the top photograph was then sold to Glenn Wood and John Lauck in 1946. They redesigned it and named it Loc-Wood Dock, seen here in 1947.

The *Tuscumbia* was one of the more popular speedboats operating out of Loc-Wood Dock in the 1940s and 50s. Another excursion boat operated by Loc-Wood was the *Grand Glaize*. The *Tuscumbia* carried 55 passengers, and the *Grand Glaize* carried 36. Seaplanes began operating in 1947. Today the *Tom Sawyer*, a double-decker paddle-wheeler, is popular at the dock.

There have been many excursion boats at the lake over the years. This 1950s photo by Massie shows the *Larry Don*, which began operation in 1948. It had a two hundred-passenger capacity when first put into service. The owner, Lawrence Fry, named the boat after his son Larry and younger brother Don. Excursions are still given on this boat, now called the *Captain Larry Don*.

Four

LAKE OZARK

"Lake Ozark is a child of Bagnell Dam and the resulting Lake of the Ozarks," reported a local newspaper in 1981. "Resorts, shops and other business places began sprouting up as the tourist trade grew on the Lake."

When the dam was under construction, several temporary towns sprang up downstream from the dam. Damsite was the largest. It was on the property of Henry and Rebecca Strange. People leased property from the Strange family, put up hastily constructed buildings, and opened businesses. As Gaylord Strange, who remembers those days, claimed: "The hills and valleys were full of tents and small buildings for which they paid three dollars a month rent."

When Bagnell Dam was finished, many of these entrepreneurs moved up to the west end of the dam and re-opened their businesses. Union Electric also encouraged business there by building the Lakeside Casino restaurant and putting in an excursion boat service.

Lake Ozark has grown in leap-frog fashion along Hwy 54 over the years. It was not incorporated until the 1960s.

Very few of the early buildings are still standing and in use, and the generation who pioneered tourism along the Lake Ozark "Strip" is largely deceased. New generations have arrived, but memories of the first generation linger in the stories they handed down to their children.

This chapter on Lake Ozark is illustrated by photographs from the Missouri State Archives and the author's collection.

In 1932, Bruce J. Duffy, from Kansas City, leased the Diamond Filling Station, one of the early filling stations in Lake Ozark, and turned it into Bruce's Ozark Inn. The inn had a dining room and dance annex. When they opened, dances were advertised as free. Duffy had experience in catering the patrons of clubs and hotels in the Kansas City area.

In 1935, the Lake Ozark "Strip" had businesses mostly along the right side going west. In this early street scene, Gordon Drug is the first business on the right. The Mobile gas station building sign says "Lake Ozark Service Station." In the distance, a water tower is under construction on top of the E.R. Smith ice plant.

By 1936, the water tower on the ice plant was complete, its sign welcoming visitors to Lake Ozark. The Lake Ozark Service Station had become Hackerman's Cottage Camp. The street, which is U.S. Highway 54, had received a coat of oil. In the 1930s, many places on the Strip sold liquor or beer and sponsored dances. As a consequence, Lake Ozark gained a short-lived reputation as a "honky-tonk" town.

The town's reputation for being wild was much exaggerated, old timers maintain. The Lake Ozark Post Office was established June 2, 1932, and was located in this small white building for several years. The first postmaster was Frank Verner Andrews, who is said to have been the person who named Lake Ozark.

School of the Osage was constructed in 1933–34 using short-term bonds and a Public Works Administration (WPA) grant. The English-style building was occupied in 1934–35. The school district was a consolidation of the Bagnell and Pleasant Grove school districts north of the dam. Before these buildings were erected, students attended classes in a building in Lakeside Village near the Holiday House.

The White House Hotel, which can be seen in both of the previous street scenes, was built on the Strip in 1932, by George Riley DeGraffenreid. He was a road construction foreman during the building of Bagnell Dam. The White House, as it is generally called, was a substantial investment, providing hotel rooms, a gas station, and café.

From left to right in this street scene is the U.S. post office in a new rock building constructed by Frank Andrews, the postmaster; next is the Overfelt Grocery, then the Osage Garage, and Standard filling station. Note the tall, visible gas bowl, gravity-flow pumps, which came into vogue in the 1920s and remained commonplace until the early 1940s.

This aerial view of the Strip, c. 1940, shows that nearly all the businesses were on one side of the road. "Lake Ozark...composed of a single row of...buildings, hotels, restaurants, dance halls, taverns and shops...is a roadside hamlet catering to vacationists," reported a 1941 WPA guidebook. "The left side of the highway, too steep to support buildings without expensive foundation construction, is unused."

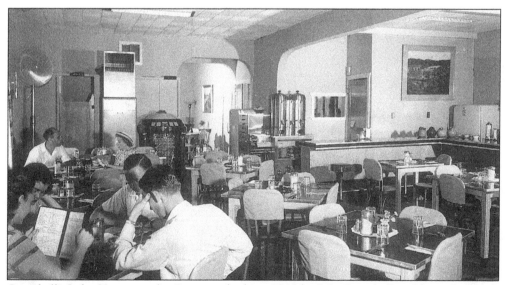

Campbell's Lake House on the Strip was built in 1946 by J.A. Campbell and his wife, Jewel. Their building was so close to the highway that the state property line came within a few feet of their front door. In 1946, they added a motel. This 1949 view of the dining room shows one of Jewel Campbell's paintings, but unfortunately, not her 30-foot wall mural. She was an accomplished artist.

SPECIALIZING IN
CAT FISH, CHICKEN, AND T-BONE
STEAK DINNERS

MR. & MRS. V. (RED) MOORE, PROPS.

LAKE OZARK,   MISSOURI

V. "Red" Moore and his wife, Carrie, were early entrepreneurs of the Strip. In 1932, they operated the Union Lunch Shop and bus station, and in 1933, they built this rock café located next to the White House Hotel. The café burned in 1939, and they then built another building closer to the dam and opened the V. "Red" Moore Gift shop.

The Conrad Motel was built in the mid-1940s by Edward Conrad on property where Herbert Hackerman's Copper Kettle stood until it burned in 1943. Although rock buildings were in vogue in the 1930s and '40s, they were also perceived as being safer. Fire was an ever-present threat to the businesses along the Strip in the early years.

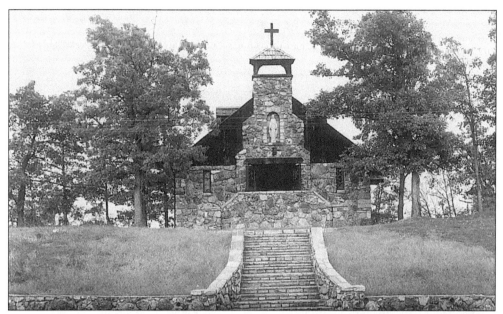

One of the early landmarks of the Lake Ozark area was Our Lady of the Lake Catholic Church, built atop a small hill about a 1.5 miles west of the dam in 1942. A wooden cross on top of the church was lit with blue neon and became a nighttime landmark for boaters. In the 1960s, this building was replaced by a larger church facility.

In 1946, Walt and Ada Tietmeyer from Nebraska built the Dogpatch Reptile Gardens and Hillbilly Farm. It became a landmark attraction on the Strip and was a forerunner of today's theme park. A reptile garden was featured in the early years and, for a time, the attraction even had a lion in a cage out front.

Arrowhead Lodge, another landmark of the Lake Ozark area, was built in 1935 by Arthur J. Kelly Jr. of Kansas City. It sits upon a hilltop overlooking the 16-mile marker of the lake, although by highway, the lodge is only 2 miles west of Bagnell Dam. The resort hotel was made of rough-hewn wood and logs. This structure burned in January of 1950 but it was later rebuilt.

Arrowhead Lodge is noted for its rustic interior. Arthur Kelly's wife was recognized in Kansas City as a gardener and antique collector. The landscaping became her responsibility, and she also dedicated several rooms in the lodge to an antique shop. The lodge has had several owners since the Kelly's but still retains its original charm.

58

One of the sheltered coves that break the bluff line at the end of the Palisades along the lake shore near the 17-mile mark is where W.W. Gore, a mechanical engineer from Madison, Wisconsin, built Gore's Boat Yard in 1932. Gore would later acquire the ferry boat *Governor McClurg* and transform it into the *Governor McClurg Show Boat*.

By 1946, when the Gore family sold their boat yard to Jack and Pee Wee Rutledge, the face of the boat yard from the water had taken on a bright and prosperous image. Rutledge renamed the establishment Port Arrowhead, long noted for its road sign with a real boat sitting atop sign poles stretching high in the air near its highway turnoff.

Islands of various sizes exist on the lake, many of them too small for any practical use. Drum Rock, shown here, is simply a novelty. Islands large enough to build on quickly became pricey real estate after the lake was formed.

The Palisades is a towering bluff line 150 feet high that extends unbroken for 2 miles along the lake shore and forms a great sweeping curve. This winter view from the Gerald Massie collection in the Missouri State Archives shows a portion of the Palisades.

Five

OSAGE BEACH

The boundary between Lake Ozark and Osage Beach lies just west of the junction of U.S. Highway 54 and Business 54 on the Miller–Camden county line. Osage Beach straddles the highway going west for a distance of 8.5 miles with Lake of the Ozarks State Park and the Grand Glaize Bridge recreational areas as major focal points.

Osage Beach, named for a man-made sand beach on the banks of the Osage River at the foot of a steep hill, had a slow beginning. It was proposed as early as 1928, by real estate promoters who platted the town and began selling lots when the dam was under construction. Unfortunately, the Great Depression made it difficult to sell lots. Most of the development of Osage Beach was between State Highway 42 and the Grand Glaize Bridge until the late 1950s, when the area began to develop rapidly. However, before this, two small historic town sites lay to the west between Osage Beach and Linn Creek—these were the towns of Zebra and Damsel. As late as 1955, Damsel was shown on highway maps. Zebra, originally along the Osage River, was named for the stripped appearance of nearby river bluffs. Today, neither Damsel nor Zebra exist. Both have been incorporated into Osage Beach, which is unquestionably one of the lake's most prosperous tourist areas.

This chapter is illustrated with photographs from the collections of Daniel Lane, John Bradbury, Missouri State Archives, AmerenUE, and the author.

The town of Zebra was originally a row of businesses on the banks of the Osage River. After the lake filled, the post office was relocated to Highway 54 in this structure, which was 20 feet long and 12 feet wide. The postmaster was a Mr. Tuttle, who may be one of the men in this 1929 photograph. By 1936, the name had been changed to Osage Beach.

Tuttle built this imposing landmark almost upon the same site as the Zebra post office, after the new Osage Beach post office building was erected further east along Highway 54. Often called "Tuttle's Tower," it was the selling site for many lake lots and other Zebra real estates ventures. The business was actually called the Buena Vista Hotel. The structure no longer exists.

To the east of Tuttle's Tower was Cannady's Café. A.B. Cannady came to the lake area in 1932 and built the café in 1933. The Cannadys were active community boosters. The early meetings of the Grand Glaize-Osage Beach Chamber of Commerce were held in this dining room. Members of this group founded the Lake of the Ozarks Association.

62

One of the more interesting "characters" among the entrepreneurs of the early days was Harry Frack. He and his first wife, Olive, built a store in Lake Ozark in the early 1930s, and in 1937, built "Frack's Acre" in Osage Beach. It included a meat market, grocery store, pottery store, ice and cold storage, beer parlor, sandwich shop, and barber shop.

Franklin's Osage Beach Hotel, originally called Franklin's Osage Beach Tavern, may have been the area's only two-story cobblestone building. B. Ray Franklin built the hotel in 1932. He was a prominent newspaper man from Jefferson City and spent $40,000 on the 23-room hotel. Electricity was furnished by a huge diesel engine. The hotel's mantle rock was a sandstone block 12 feet long and 7 inches thick from Ha Ha Tonka.

Lake of the Ozarks State Park borders the Grand Glaize arm of the Lake of the Ozarks and comprises more than 17,000 forested acres with trails, beaches, playgrounds, and other recreational facilities. Union Electric transferred the land to the federal government in 1935–1937, and the park was developed with the help of the Civilian Conservation Corps.

Water skiing originated in the 1920s. Some skiing was done at the lake in the late 1930s, but it wasn't until the '50s that the passion for water skiing truly developed at the lake. Kirkwood Lodge established a water ski school, complete with jumping ramps. Eventually, performance skiing spawned ski shows at the lake.

Pla-Port Resort, built on a high point of land overlooking the junction of the Osage and Grand Glaize Rivers, is a vanished landmark of regal status. The resort was built in 1932 by L.A. Kelly. The crowning feature of the resort was its lighthouse, rising 130 feet above the lake. It was for many years the only privately operated lighthouse on any inland lake in the United States.

Featuring guest rooms and dance pavilion, the Spanish-style, medieval-appearing structure was designed by H.T. Forrester. A rotating green and white light installed in the tower could be seen upon the lake for a distance of 14 miles. Pla-Port's lighthouse was in operation for a number of years, until a lightning strike destroyed its equipment.

LAKE OF THE OZARKS, SEEN FROM HILDEBRAND'S

"DAYDREAMING" AND A TYPICAL COTTAGE AT HILDEBRAND'S
LOCATION: LAKE ROAD 24 AND U. S. HIGHWAY 54
POST OFFICE AND TELEPHONE CENTRAL: OSAGE BEACH, MO.

Another resort of early vintage in the Osage Beach area is Hildebrand's. Originally called Hilterbrand's Camp, it was built in 1936 by Reinhart Hiltebrand and his sister. The card shown here has a "Shepherd of the Hills" character. The scenery at the southwest end of the majestic Palisades where Hiltebrand Resort is located is superb. Hiltebrand's sister was an accomplished painter and sold her work at the resort.

Hildebrand's Resort was noted for its wading pool, its "honeymoon" trail along the Palisades, and for water skiing. Still a novelty in the late 1930s, Hildebrand called water skiing "walking on the water" and promoted it as a "unique recreation."

66

Creating Lake of the Ozarks necessitated a bridge across the Grand Glaize Creek at Zebra to carry U.S. Highway 54. In this 1929 photo, bridge construction is just getting under way at the next bend of the stream up the valley. Behind the photographer, it is only a short distance to the junction of the Glaize with the Osage River. A cow path meanders along the valley floor below the bluff and hillside.

The bridge was designed and built by Sverdrup and Parcel, consulting engineers from St. Louis. By the fall of 1930, all six of the high piers were in place, and the bridge was beginning to take shape. For scale, two workers can be seen standing on top of the steel work just above the second pier.

By December 1, 1930, the steel superstructure of the Grand Glaize Bridge was complete but Bagnell Dam was not, so there was no water beneath the bridge. The framing structure was built below the deck and not above it, so that people would have an unimpeded view of the lake. This unusual feature quickly gave it a nickname—the Upside Down Bridge.

The Grand Glaize Bridge is 1,630 feet long and has been a celebrated attraction since it was built. By the 1970s, growth of tourism in the lake area was bringing so many people to the lake that the bridge could barely handle the traffic load. Its concrete deck was also deteriorating, so a twin bridge was built beside it in 1984, and the decking for this span was replaced in 1990.

This aerial view of the Grand Glaize Bridge shows development at both ends in the 1950s. It also demonstrates why this bridge provides one of the most scenic crossings of the Lake of the Ozarks. Today it is one of the busiest recreational focal points in the entire lake region.

Chester Mason "Chet" Hymes built Chet's Anchor Inn at the east end of the Grand Glaize Bridge in the 1940s. He kept adding to his business at the water's edge until it looked like an amusement park. Chet eventually sold, and built a restaurant and go-kart track along Highway 54 further east. The site in this photo then became known as Links Landing.

The Grand Glaize Cafe serving fish could be found at the west end of the Grand Glaize Bridge until it was eventually sold and became a steak house known as the Potted Steer. Rumor has it that the first building on this site was a fisherman's shack which was moved up from the river's edge when construction began on the Grand Glaize Bridge.

Many different excursion boats have operated at the Grand Glaize Bridge since the 1930s. The *Idle Time*, a 21-ton steel boat, operated during the 1940s. In May 1951, it was taken out of the lake and put back into the water below Bagnell Dam. Elwood Hibarger of Wichita piloted it down the Osage, Missouri, and Mississippi Rivers, then up the Red River to Lake Tecoma, Texas, to begin service there as an excursion boat.

Of all the dance cruise boats to operate at the Grand Glaize Bridge, none are as fondly remembered as the *Governor McClurg Show Boat*. Named for the most famous merchant of the Osage River valley during the 19th century, the *Governor McClurg* began to serve in the 1930s as a car ferry on the lake before the construction of the Niangua and Hurricane Deck bridges on Highway 5 north of Camdenton.

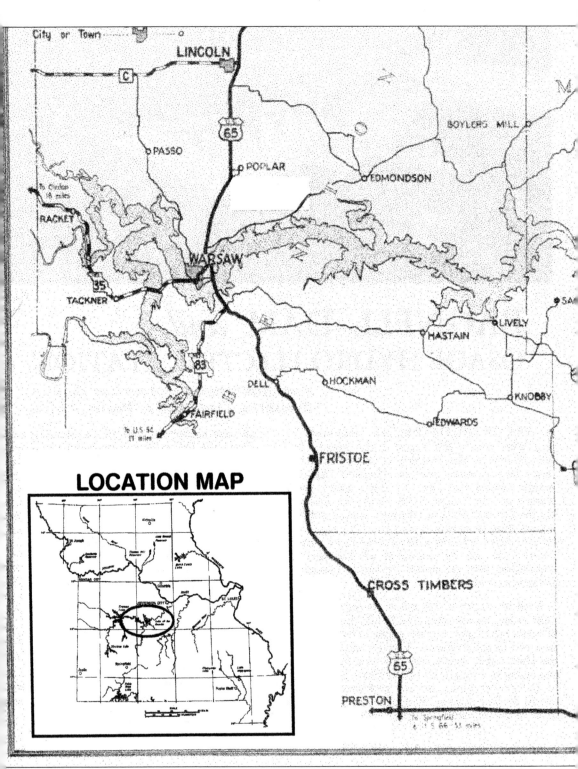

This map is based on a similar map published in 1939 by the Union Electric Land and Development Company, which was dissolved in the 1940s. The map has been modified to show

certain features mentioned in this book such as major bridges and certain towns not shown on the 1939 map. The map was modified for the author by Susan Dunn of Rolla, Missouri.

Outdoor sports, recreation, amusements, beautiful scenery and clean country life
are the contributions of

THE LAKE OF THE OZARKS
to the vacation life of nature-loving Americans

Photos of fish catches by lucky fishermen dominated the advertising of resorts and camps at Lake of the Ozarks in the 1930s and '40s. This gradually gave way to photos of recreational pastimes such as water skiing, swimming, sun bathing, and boating. Fishing is still popular in some areas of the lake, and tournaments are common.

From 10,000 feet some people see the profile of the lake as a great dragon. This photo was taken by the late Gerald Massie. The dragon theme has been promoted at the lake since the early 1930s, and the area's promotional mascot today is a dragon.

74

Six

LINN CREEK

Linn Creek is located in a valley along U.S. Highway 54, 3 miles northeast of Camdenton. The site of "Old" Linn Creek is farther down the valley and was inundated when Lake of the Ozarks was created.

Old Linn Creek was platted in 1845 on the banks of the Osage River near the confluence of the Niangua and Osage Rivers and the creek for which the town was named. It became an important steamboat shipping port.

The town began when John Jones, the brother-in-law of Joseph McClurg, settled at the site in 1845 and opened a store. He was joined there in 1852 by McClurg. Jones died a couple of years later in an explosion of the steamboat *Kit Kearney*. McClurg continued by building and operating steamboats, packing and shipping meats, and smelting and shipping lead. He became a leader not only in his community but a noted politician. He served four years as a U.S. congressman from the 5th Congressional District and was elected governor of Missouri in 1868.

The citizens of Linn Creek were bitterly divided over the construction of Bagnell Dam and where to relocate their beloved town in 1930. Some moved their homes up the valley to where modern-day Linn Creek is located. Some moved to the surrounding hills, while the remainder moved to the present-day site of Camdenton, which became the new county seat.

This chapter is illustrated with photos from the collections of the Camden County Historical Society, Daniel Lane, AmerenUE, and the author.

When steamboats began to ply the Osage River after 1840, the river quickly earned a reputation for being as treacherous as the Missouri River. As shipping increased, it became necessary for dredge boats to operate on the river. They worked to clear the river of shoals, rocks, trees, and submerged logs. In this case, the dredge boat was probably also the home of its operator.

The main street of "Upper Town" in Old Linn Creek is pictured about 1920. Automobiles were common enough for the Moulder Garage to prosper. The automobile sitting in front of the garage is next to a curbside. gravity-fed fuel pump that dispenses Red Crown gasoline. The Moulders were one of the pioneer families of Camden County and Old Linn Creek.

Linn Creek had some fine homes in the upper part of town. The home of Dr. Moore is said to have been the first with a bathtub. It was one of the houses not to be demolished, and soon after this photo was taken, the house was moved to save it from the lake waters.

When originally founded, Old Linn Creek had an "Upper Town" and "Lower Town." Although Lower Town, which was developed around the steamboat landing, was a place of commerce, Upper Town also developed and prospered as people moved away from the flood-prone areas to higher ground.

When a steamboat docked, it was always an occasion for excitement. Before docking, the pilot would sound the ship's loud whistle, and people would hurry to the boat landing. The *Scout* was just one of many boats that stopped at Old Linn Creek. Others included the *Homer C. Wright*, the *Flora Jones*, *J.R. Wells*, *John R. Hugo*, the *Frederick*, and the *Otter*.

Home of Gov. McClurge
Lake of the Ozarks

The private home of Joseph W. McClurg, not far from the Old Linn Creek suspension bridge, stood just a few feet above the elevation of 660—full reservoir level of Lake of the Ozarks. The McClurg home was allowed to stand, even though the water came close to it. Through the 1930s, it was operated as a hotel. It was destroyed by fire in the 1940s.

Joseph W. McClurg retired from public life in 1894, and lived with his daughter and son-in-law, C.C. Draper. "He became a familiar and loved figure with his long, white beard, quaint old fashioned dress, and dignified, courteous and cheerful bearing," said his great granddaughter Emma Gibbs Phillips. McClurg died December 2, 1900, and is buried in the Lebanon, Missouri, cemetery.

At the confluence of the Niangua and Osage Rivers at Old Linn Creek, a ferry carried commerce across the water. The first ferry at this location was the *Aaron Crain* ferry, licensed April 12, 1841. The ferry shown here is the *Harvey Kiplinger* ferry, the last ferry to operate at Old Linn Creek.

The southeastern approach to the Old Linn Creek suspension bridge took one to the bluff top and the toll house. The northwestern end of the bridge across the river exited onto cultivated bottom lands. The two-story toll house can be seen at the top of the hill.

The Old Linn Creek suspension bridge was built across the Osage River in 1911 by T.S. Hart, who was reared near Old Linn Creek. He had no engineering background or formal training in such work, having learned the trade by simply doing it. Before building the Linn Creek bridge, he had constructed a bridge across the Auglaize at Zebra.

Although born and raised near Old Linn Creek, T.S. Hart had been living in Moniteau County before building the Old Linn Creek suspension bridge. He built a substantial house on the cliff side of the river, and it became the Hart home as well as a place of business—the toll house. He charged farmers $10 a year to use the bridge.

The "Old Linn Creek Swinger," as the bridge was fondly called, received a great deal of acclaim in its day. Its destruction very nearly gave it legendary status. Instead of letting the bridge be salvaged, the men who destroyed it for the dam builders simply let it fall into the river. Many different postcard views of the bridge can still be found in circulation.

Dr. Moore's house is pictured being readied for movement up the valley to a new site. Many houses were moved and placed on new foundations in both "New" Linn Creek and Camdenton, including the residences of Pope, Lewis, Watson, King, Jefferies, Woolery, and Osborn.

In this aerial photo, taken February 2, 1931, a large percentage of the structures in Old Linn Creek have been demolished. Those that were not moved by their owners were torched by the men doing the clearing. Many people of the community stood in tears as they watched their homes go up in flames. Old Linn Creek has achieved legendary status in the lake area.

While the destruction of most of the buildings in Old Linn Creek was occasioned by sadness, the destruction of at least one building brought some light-hearted moments for everyone—the demolition of the jail. The first jail in Camden County was built before the Civil War, but the one from which this metal cage came was a much, much later version.

There were many places of beauty and fond memories in the valleys of the Niangua and Osage Rivers that were lost to the lake. The site of Arnhold's Mill, owned by Dorotha and George Arnold on the Big Niangua, was one. Dating from the late 1870s, the mill site was a favorite of sportsmen from throughout the state.

The Great Stone Face was a projecting bluff of dolomite rock with the profile of an Indian's face. It was a landmark for river boatmen, and was certainly a favorite subject for early photographers and the makers of postcard images. The valleys of the Osage and Niangua are steeped in Indian legend.

The site of Chimney Rock along the Osage River was another landmark that the natives of Old Linn Creek hated to lose, especially the fishermen. It is said that fishing was exceptionally good along the base of this bluff. The Osage River has chiseled itself deeply into the bedrock of the Ozarks, and many bluffs still survive to beautify Lake of the Ozarks.

Above Old Linn Creek, at the crest of the highest bluff, are the gnarled rocks of Lovers Leap. These sentinels of time watched Old Linn Creek grow, prosper, and then disappear beneath the waters of the lake. Though the rocks remain unchanged, the vista which they overlook has certainly changed, but remains one of beauty.

Forty feet of water covers it all today. No, you can't see the buildings of Old Linn Creek when the water is low, because they were all torn down. Legends and tall tales about Old Linn Creek live on among the boaters of today but they are nothing but that—stories to entertain people who enjoy a mystery from before their time.

The Osage River town that refused to die became two towns—"New" Linn Creek, or just Linn Creek as we know it today, and Camdenton. This 1930s view of Linn Creek shows two arches, now gone. They proclaim Linn Creek to be the southern gateway to the lake.

Seven

CAMDENTON

Camdenton officially became the new county seat of Camden County in November 1930, when the county records were moved from Old Linn Creek to the new town site. The site was originally a part of the Chapman farm. Approximately 160 acres were purchased for the new town site by Clint Webb on January 16, 1930, for $2,750, and the work of clearing the land and laying out the new town began immediately. Webb and his partner, Jim Banner, held an auction soon after a deep well was installed, to sell lots. The crowd was treated to a free barbecue, and to assure the people that the town site had good water, the well water was served as drinks. At the center of town, the road from Old Linn Creek divided, one leading to Ha Ha Tonka and the other to Lebanon.

The town grew quickly and by April of 1932, the local paper recorded that the town had 67 dwellings, 2 churches, a Masonic Lodge, a new court house, a new consolidated high school, 2 hotels, 2 cafes, 2 barber shops, 2 garages, 4 general stores, 1 ice plant, 1 drug store, 1 bank, 1 newspaper, 1 airport, 1 lumber yard, 1 jewelry store, 1 electric shop, 1 abstract and title company, and 9 other businesses including tourist camps, service stations, a pool hall, and a plumber's shop. Camdenton also had a water and sewer system and electricity from the M&E Hydro-electric Plant on the Niangua River.

This chapter is illustrated with photos from the collections of Daniel Lane, Missouri State Archives, and the author.

Camdenton is located at the junction of U.S. Highway 54 and Missouri State Highway 5. This aerial photo dates to the 1940s. The town soon acquired a couple of nicknames—the "Miracle City" and the "Hub City of the Ozarks." The latter nickname stuck and was often used in promotional literature for the first 50 years of the town's history.

The first courthouse built in Old Linn Creek was erected in 1867. It burned in 1902. The building in the lower left photo above is the structure that replaced it. This building was torn down during the demolition of Old Linn Creek, and a new courthouse was erected in Camdenton (top photo) in 1932.

The Ozark Tavern Hotel, built on the Camdenton square in early 1932 by Boyd W. Harwood and his son, Boyd W. Jr. of Kansas City, began as just a 12-room hotel. Business was so good that by the fall of the same year, they doubled the size of their establishment. The word "tavern" was dropped in the mid-1940s.

In this early photo taken on the Camdenton "hub" or square by Gerald Massie, a Missouri State Highway Patrol officer keeps an eye on traffic at the intersection. In the background is the Moulder Hotel and Coffee Shop. In the foreground, the signpost gives mileage to destination points on U.S. Highway 54 and State Highway 5.

One of the early attractions in Camdenton was Wilkerson's Figure Bottle Museum next to Cedar Grove Cottages along Highway 54. It was owned and operated by Maude Wilkerson. The building, of native stone, included a wide variety of rocks including formations taken from local caves. The nearby cottages were also native stone structures.

Among the first hotel-café combinations in Camdenton was the Curtright Hotel and Café, built in the distinctive "giraffe rock" style. All throughout the lake in the 1930s and '40s, giraffe rock and cobblestone buildings were common. The stone in this building is largely native sandstone obtained locally about four miles west of Camdenton off U.S. Highway 54.

The café with probably the best lake view in the Camdenton area was the Cave Inn off Highway 5 North, at the top of the hill above Bridal Cave overlooking the Big Niangua arm of Lake of the Ozarks.

More than two hundred wild caves are known in the Lake of the Ozarks area, and many other caves were inundated by the lake. Some caves were transformed into show caves around the perimeter of the lake beginning in 1932. Bridal Cave, 2 miles west of Camdenton on the shoreline of the Big Niangua arm of the lake, was opened in 1948 by B.F. Krehbiel, R.L. Wilkerson, and Jim Banner.

Bridal Cave is the only operating show cave in the lake area that is right on the shoreline of the lake. The cave entrance is partway up the side of Thunder Mountain. The cave can be reached by either car or boat. This photo by the late Eddie Miller, who managed the cave for many years, shows the first boat dock built below the cave entrance. The cave tour is a walking tour.

Bridal Cave acquired its name before the beginning of the 20th century, based on a legend of an Indian wedding at the cave. Since being opened to the public, more than 1,500 weddings have been held in the cave's natural bridal chapel. Bill Mason, of Versailles, was the wedding photographer for many years.

The Bridal Cave Development Co. also bought Coakley Cave, 7 miles east of Highway 54 and Linn Creek on State Route A. They opened the cave in 1952, naming it Ozark Caverns. It is now owned by Lake of the Ozarks State Park. Jim Banner (on the right), one of the founders of Camdenton, is shown in this photo before the cave's first ticket building. With him are the Logans. who managed the cave.

A goldfish pond was built in the spacious entrance area but was not fed by the cave stream, which can be seen beneath the boardwalk. The pond was fed by a small spring which originates along the left side of the entrance chamber.

Both Ozark Caverns and Bridal Cave are known for their spectacular cave formations. This photo in Ozark Caverns shows the "Angels' Shower," a cave formation complex unique to the cave. Although the falling water can barely be discerned in this photo, a rain of water pours continuously from the center of the overhead stalactites to keep the natural crystal basin on the floor full and overflowing with spring water.

The Niangua Bridge a few miles west of Camdenton carries U.S. Highway 54 over the lake. Downstream, a few miles to the left, is Bridal Cave. To the right, upstream, is the famed Ha Ha Tonka area. Not visible in this photo is the entrance to Bunch Cave in the hillside that is to the left of the bridge. Bunch Cave was operated as a show cave in 1938 and 1939, and called Big Niangua Cave.

Tonka Villa Resort was at the east end of the bridge. It was from this resort that tour boats left for a visit to Big Niangua Cave in the late 1930s The villa no longer exists. The eastern approach to the new Niangua Bridge has claimed its location.

Lowell's Boat Docks and Resort operated on the downstream side at the west end of the Niangua Bridge. The resort was only a few hundred feet from the entrance to Big Niangua Cave, yet the tours were operated by the owners of a resort on the opposite side of the lake.

In the 1940s and '50s, square dancing was very popular at the lake. Camdenton was a square dance center. This photo, by Gerald Massie, was taken at Lake Park Marina in the 1950s. The marina, owned and operated by Buford and Anna May Foster, is upstream from the west end of the Niangua Bridge.

Eight

HA HA TONKA

The mystique of Ha Ha Tonka is its blend of natural wonders and cultural artifacts. All of the ingredients of fact, fiction, romance, and adventure are here upon a 2,700-acre tract of land. It could have been Missouri's first state park in 1911, but it did not become a state park until 1978. In the book *Exploring Missouri's Legacy, State Parks and Historic Sites*, editor Susan Flader writes: "No other state park has a more fascinating, if convoluted, history, Indians, early explorers, frontiersmen, outlaws, turn-of-the-century capitalists, and twentieth century real estate speculators…"

Dr. Walter Williams, founder of the Missouri School of Journalism, smitten with the beauty of Ha Ha Tonka and exaggerating a bit, proclaimed in the early 1900s that it contained more natural curiosities than in any other similar share of the earth's surface. "If Hahatonka were on a railroad it would have thousands of visitors where now it has one…." said Williams.

No train has ever carried visitors to the foot of the Ha Ha Tonka bluffs, but good roads now lead people to this wondrous place by the thousands every year. It has become one of Missouri's most popular state parks, and is located off U.S. Highway 54 just south of Camdenton on the Big Niangua arm of Lake of the Ozarks. For sheer beauty and historical intrigue it has no equal elsewhere in Missouri.

This chapter is illustrated with photos from the collections of Daniel Lane, Van Beydler, James Martin, Missouri State Archives, and the author.

Ha Ha Tonka Castle is pictured as it appeared in the 1930s above the great chasm and Lake of the Ozarks.

The natural history of Ha Ha Tonka began when groundwater and surface water ate away at the bedrock, forming sinkholes, caves, springs, hills, and a natural bridge. In the process a huge cave passage collapsed, forming a wide chasm a half-mile long, with walls of rock 250 feet high. In the center of the chasm is a cave-riddled island, and at the head is Ha Ha Tonka Spring, discharging 48 million gallons of water daily.

The spring water forms a lake in the canyon, and then divides around the island to rejoin at the mouth of the chasm and flows immediately into Lake of the Ozarks. Before the Lake of the Ozarks was formed, the spring branch flowed to the Niangua River. In the winters of 1801 and 1802, Daniel Boone and his son Nathan trapped beaver here.

The Osage Indians claimed this magnificent place and would let other Indian tribes, particularly those from the western plains, camp at Ha Ha Tonka in the winter. Place names of the locale are of Indian origin. The Osage and Niangua Rivers take their names from the Indians, as does Ha Ha Tonka itself. The words Ha Ha Tonka mean "laughing waters."

The great Balanced Rock of Ha Ha Tonka, estimated to weigh 150 tons, is pictured here as it appeared in the early 1900s. The rock was standing sentinel when Lieutenant James B. Wilkinson of the Pike Expedition described the region in his report. This was also around the time when a band of outlaws set up a hideout inside the caves of the chasm and established a counterfeiting operation in the 1830s.

No photo is known of the first grist mill at Ha Ha Tonka. It was erected in the 1830s by Garland, a counterfeiter, and used as a front for his illegal activities. The mill shown in the two photos on this page was built by Tom Garrison in 1869, and stood until 1930, when it was burned by the men who were clearing land for the Lake of the Ozarks.

Tom Garrison dammed the spring branch near its junction with the Niangua River, creating a lake that became quite popular for fishing. An early report of the Missouri Bureau of Labor Statistics praised the lake, saying that it was the largest spring-fed lake in Missouri, and that it was "a beautiful body of water covering an area of 90 acres, and from 40 to 60 feet deep."

Trout were introduced to the lake in the chasm at a fairly early date, and trout fishing became a popular attraction. These fishermen are working the swift, cold spring waters of the Trout Glen on the north side of the island in the Ha Ha Tonka chasm. The year is 1911.

Hunting game in the hills of Ha Ha Tonka was also popular in the early days. The last bear killed in Camden County was hunted down in Bear Cave at Ha Ha Tonka in the 1880s. The Frisco Railroad, which passed through Lebanon 40 miles to the east, promoted Tonka as a good site for sporting activities along the Frisco route. This photo was taken from inside the Natural Bridge.

Cave exploring was another attraction at Ha Ha Tonka. The large entrance to River Cave opens at the base of a deep sinkhole in the sinkhole-littered landscape east of the castle and chasm. Large chambers characterize the cave, which has about three-fourths of a mile of explorable passage. Eyeless, albino salamanders were discovered in the cave in the 1800s and created a great deal of scientific interest.

Known originally as Berry Cave, River Cave was shown commercially as Mystic River Cave in the late 1940s and through the '50s. The large stalagmite column in this photo is known as the "Christmas Tree." One of the early owners of the property was so fond of this cave formation that he planned to remove the stalagmite and display it in a museum. Fortunately, his ambition was never realized.

It was a hunting trip that introduced Robert M. Snyder, a wealthy businessman from Kansas City, to the site in 1903. Captivated, he purchased 60 tracts of land and proceeded to build a private retreat with the crown jewel being a huge, European-style, castle-like mansion atop the bluff overlooking the chasm. Stone and timber used in the construction of the 23-room castle were all taken from the property.

Construction materials were hauled to the castle site on a miniature railroad. The estate also included an elaborate stable and carriage house on the bluff top. Greenhouses were located behind the castle, and to the right of the carriage house was the water tower. Unfortunately, Robert Snyder did not live to see the castle finished. He died in a car wreck in 1906, and all work on the property stopped.

During construction, the steep slope above the bluff and spring was nearly denuded of vegetation, but in time cedar trees grew to cover the bare ground. This view from the unfinished castle shows the carriage house and water tower.

This view, from the front of the castle about 1908, was taken when the grounds lay devoid of activity. Their jobs gone, the workers went home. The stonemasons Snyder had brought from Scotland returned to their native land. However, in 1922, the Snyder sons returned to Ha Ha Tonka to complete their father's dream.

The view from the top of the Ha Ha Tonka water tower is great. Originally, there were several floors in the tower and a stairway going to the top where a large water tank was installed. The tower was part of the water system, where water for the castle was pumped up from the spring in the chasm. There were guest rooms in the tower for a time. This photo shows the tower as it appeared in the 1920s.

The greenhouses were both extensive and elaborate. They were very nearly complete when Snyder died. The glass was never installed in most of the frames. Today, only a few foundation stones remain to show where the greenhouses once stood.

The Snyder sons did not have their father's wealth, but they did complete the mansion and used it for a number of years as a private retreat. When Bagnell Dam was built, the waters of Lake of the Ozarks backed up the spring branch and destroyed Ha Ha Tonka Lake. The Snyders sued Union Electric for damages and settled out of court for $200,000.

In time, vegetation reclaimed the slopes, and the grounds took on the lushness of the Ozark region in which they are located. This view from the water tower was taken about 1940.

This photo, taken from the hill opposite Deer's Leap Hill upon which the castle stands, is where the small settlement of Ha Ha Tonka once stood. It was platted in 1883 by L.J. Roach and Alfred Garrison, and named Gunter. The Ha Ha Tonka Spring was briefly owned by a man named Gunter in the 1840s, and for a time the spring was also known as Gunter's Spring.

A guest room in the Ha Ha Tonka Castle is pictured above. In 1936, the Snyders leased the castle for use as a vacation hotel and resort. It was managed by Josephine Ellis.

This was the dining room in Ha Ha Tonka Castle. In 1942, sparks from a fireplace kindled a fire among the mansion's wooden shingles, and the castle was soon gutted by fire. The fire was so hot that even the shingles on the carriage house caught fire, and it too was lost.

The post office at Ha Ha Tonka was called Gunter Springs until the 1890s. Maggie Lodge, whose husband was Lt. Thomas W. Lodge, was the first postmaster. She was able to get the name of the spring and post office changed to the Indian name—Ha Ha Tonka. The post office remained in service until 1932.

One of the first resorts to spring up adjacent to the Ha Ha Tonka estate was Lakeside, located on a strip of land between Ha Ha Tonka Lake and the Niangua River. It became a retreat for well-to-do families from Kansas City even before the 1920s. The name Ha Ha Tonka was often written as one word before the establishment of Ha Ha Tonka State Park in 1978.

After the castle burned, the property changed hands several times, each new owner trying in vain to transform the place into a profitable resort or other commercial enterprise. As time passed, rains washed away the burned look, leaving handsome ruins that quickly took on a mystic look all their own.

The combination of natural wonders and the ruins of a castle that can be seen for miles upon the crest of Deer's Leap Hill quickly transformed Ha Ha Tonka into a paradise for nature lovers, history buffs, and photographers.

This impressive aerial view of the Ha Ha Tonka ruins, chasm, and Lake of the Ozarks from the Missouri State Archives was taken by the late Gerald Massie in the 1950s.

When the Lake of the Ozarks is low, the ruins of the cave passage can be explored. Big, fallen blocks of dolomite, pitted with solution, litter the stream bed where the stream branch joins the lake. It seems ironic, yet appropriate, that the ruins of a great cave should lie in the chasm below the ruins of a great castle atop the bluff.

But the fishing is always good, they say, among the rocky ruins at Ha Ha Tonka. This Missouri State Archives photo from the collection of Gerald Massie captures some of the charm that now makes Ha Ha Tonka one of Missouri's most popular state parks and historic sites.

Nine

HURRICANE DECK TO VERSAILLES

State Highway 5 going north from Camdenton passes through some of the more scenic areas of the Lake of the Ozarks. The highway crosses the Niangua arm of the lake 9 miles north of Camdenton and then the Osage arm at 14 miles. Both bridges were designed to provide the optimum viewing pleasure.

Over the next 13 miles, travelers pass through the communities of Hurricane Deck, Sunrise Beach, and Laurie on the way to Gravois Mills. All of these settlements have sprung up since the lake was created—except for Gravois Mills.

Gravois Mills was platted in 1884. Near here, Josiah S. Walton built a water-driven gristmill in 1835. In 1870, the Hume brothers built a woolen mill in the area, and in 1895, Asa Webster purchased the property. Webster added a sawmill and built the stone dam that forms the Tourtdale Fish Hatchery, a popular attraction in the area even today.

Versailles is located on Highway 5 about 9 miles north of Gravois Mills. It has been the county seat of Morgan County since 1834. The Missouri Pacific Railroad reached the town in 1858. The community considers itself the northernmost gateway to the lake. In the late 1800s, large numbers of Swiss and German families settled around Versailles, and many of them were Mennonites. The Mennonites are still prominent among the farmers that till the prairie uplands north of Versailles.

This chapter is illustrated with photos from the collections of Daniel Lane and the author.

Sailing on Lake of the Ozarks in the 1940s at Washburn's Point near Gravois Mills is depicted here.

When the lake was filled in 1931, it severed "Old" Highway 5 at two points—where it crossed the Niangua River and the Osage River. There were no state funds available at the time to build bridges across these lake arms, so a ferry was established. It crossed the lake between the Osage Inn on the south side near the Governor McClurg Mansion, and the Floyd farm on the north side. It went into service in June 1932.

The motor ferry *Governor McClurg* was 66 feet long and 34 feet wide. It had a capacity for 19 cars and was powered with a 100-horse diesel engine. Bridges were built across the two lake arms in 1936. The ferry was then taken downlake to Gore's Boat Dock and converted to the *Governor McClurg Show Boat*. Frank Miles, who operated the boat as a ferry, stayed on to manage the excursions.

Cross the LAKE of the OZARKS
ON THE
GOVERNOR McCLURG
FERRY
PERFECTS STATE HIGHWAY NO. 5

Enjoy the pleasing experience of riding with your car across the beautiful, blue waters of the Lake of the Ozarks. "The Governor McClurg" bridges the gap in State Highway No. 5—and, now, for a mile and a quarter you ride in comfort and safety on waters that cover historic ground. You are within sight of the spot where old Linn Creek stood; now forty feet submerged. You see the abutment of the old suspension bridge. To the east on the brink of the Lake is "Old Erie," an early-day courthouse that barely escaped the rising waters. And, to the west stands the far-famed, majestic Lover's Leap. The convergence here of the Niangua river, Linn Creek and the Osage river adds to the beauty and scenic charm.

The motor ferry *Governor McClurg* was more than just a transportation business. It was also an attraction, and many people took the ride just to see the sites as they were described in this ad by the Governor McClurg Ferry Lines, which was published in the 1932 edition of *Where To Go In The Ozarks* by Keith McCanse.

This is how the view downstream from Hurricane Deck appeared in 1930 when the basin was being cleared for the lake. The faint line of hills four miles distant is where Lovers Leap and Old Linn Creek lie along the banks of the Osage River. The name Hurricane Deck comes from a 1.5-mile-long slice of high bluff along the Osage River.

One of the first fishing camps established in the Hurricane Deck area was Lone Oak Point Resort. In 1931, Charles Borel, while boating on the new lake, saw a point of land he wanted to buy for his camp, but first he had to find it by land. Since there were no roads in that location, he had to walk the woodlands until he found it. However, he didn't get cabins built until 1942.

HURRICANE DECK BRIDGE OVER OSAGE ARM
Designed by Sverdrup and Parcel, Consulting Engineers
Prize award of American Institute of Steel Construction as most beautiful bridge in its class—
Built in 1936

BRIDGE OVER NIANGUA ARM

Built by Missouri State Highway Department 1936

Designed by Sverdrup and Parcel Consulting Engineers

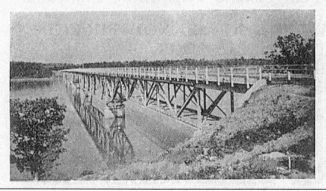

BRIDGE OVER GRAND GLAIZE ARM

Sverdrup and Parcel Consulting Engineers St. Louis, Mo.

Sverdrup and Parcel were very proud of the bridges they designed for the Lake of the Ozarks. This ad appeared in the Lake Association's 1939 Map and Resort Guide. The Hurricane Deck bridge, which cost $655,000 to build, was a toll bridge for a number of years, and when it opened, the fee for automobile and driver was 40¢ with a round-trip for 70¢.

80-TON MARINE RAILWAY, 14,000 Feet of Inside Storage

GRAVOIS BOAT and DRY DOCK CO.

Route 78, Gravois Mills, Mo.

CHRIS-CRAFT SALES and SERVICE

COMPLETE MARINE REPAIR AND PARTS SERVICE
Boat and Motor Rental and Sales Service
Operating in Connection:

GRAVOIS GRILL

SHORT ORDERS, DINNERS BY RESERVATION

GRAVOIS POINT

This ad for the Gravois Boat and Dry Dock Co. appeared in the lake area's 1939 Map and Resort Guide. The docks maintained one of the largest pleasure and fishing fleets on the lake in the late 1930s.

Two other resorts built early in the Hurricane Deck area were Green Bay Terrace Resort and Purvis Beach Resort. William Green Sr., better known as "Sittin' Bill, Chief of the Ozark Hillbillies" ran Green Bay Terrace Resort. Ivy and Ora Hill Purvis owned and operated the Purvis Beach Resort shown above.

The Purvis Beach Resort cafe building also housed the local post office. Ivy Purvis was the postmaster. A post office was first established in this north Camden County area soon after the Civil War, and was moved several times. It came to this location in 1923, where Ivy served until 1945, when she quit for health reasons. The post office was then discontinued.

Gravois Mills straddles Highway 5 for about one mile and gives the impression of a being a small fishing village. The lake roads that spiderweb off Highway 5 on both sides lead to busy resorts and camps. The Gravois Creek arm of the lake is relatively shallow, and when the water is low, the portion of the lake that can be seen along Highway 5 in this area looks marshy.

The street scene at the top of this page shows the Gravois Motel on the right. Next to the motel is the building shown here, which housed the post office, ice plant, liquor store, grocery, and café in the 1930s, '40s, and '50s.

Among the early 1930s fishing camps and resorts on the shoreline downstream from Gravois Mills were Twin Bays Camp, Rocky Comfort Lodge, Two Waters Resort, Happy Days Resort, Jester's Camp, Silver Moon Camp, Mel Adkins Camp, Cedar Point Camp, Art Sampson's Camp, and Roaring Oaks Camp.

Washburn's Point, next to Two Waters Resort, consisted initially of a clubhouse and a couple of cottages built by the Country Club of Missouri. It was purchased by Bill and Lottie Washburn in 1932. The "Point" was best known for its excellent fishing guide service.

JACOB'S CAVE

The Show Place of the Lake of the Ozarks Region

New passages in this ancient Cavern with its historic association, have recently been discovered and opened to reveal rare formations of marvelous and entrancing beauty.

Paths have been built so the Cave is easily traversed, and its amazing stalactites and aged stalagmites may be viewed by everyone in comfort and safety.

One of the Newly Opened Vaults

"I never miss an opportunity to go in an Ozark cave. Twice now I have inspected Jacob's Cave—the last trip since the openings have been made into heretofore inaccessible passages. It was a delightful trip over well-made walks with a painstaking guide to point out the unusual and absorbing formations and to tell of the history of the ages unmistakably written there. I can recommend this trip as an exhilarating underground adventure in safety as well as for its educational benefits."

—KEITH MCCANSE.

Eight caves in the lake area have been open to the public at one time or another since 1932. The first cave to be commercialized was Jacob's Cave, north of Gravois Mills on Route TT. This ad appeared in the guide book *Where to Go in the Ozarks* by Keith McCanse in 1932, and also in *Missouri Magazine*. The fee for a tour in 1932 was 25¢.

A series of five photos, later made into postcards and sold at the cave, was taken in the early 1950s by Hammond and Irwin of Jefferson City, whose photography was used by the Missouri Division of Resources and Development. This building covered the entrance and air-conditioned the gift shop. It has since burned and been replaced with a new structure.

This Hammond and Irwin photograph shows the large entrance room of the cave. Jacob's Cave was discovered in 1875 by Jacob Craftcraft, a lead miner. Russell P. Hall, a realtor, owned and operated the cave in the 1950s. It was later sold to Frank and Jane Hurley who still operate the cave. The cave is noted for its great variety of beautiful cave formations.

The business district of Versailles is built around a square, and this early street scene shows businesses along the north side. The street in this photo, c. 1910, is not yet paved. Morgan County, in which Versailles in located, was organized in 1833 and named for General Daniel Morgan, a Revolutionary War patriot.

The old Martin Hotel, a half-block north of the square, was built by Samuel Martin in 1878 and replaced a log tavern which had stood on this site since 1851. At the 26-room hotel, guests were furnished with a bed, washstand with bowl and pitcher, chair, and chamber pot. A coil of rope at a window in each guest room served as a fire escape. The building is now a museum.

In 1835, Morgan County purchased a log house at the corner of the square and used it as a courthouse. In 1844, it was replaced with a two-story brick structure in the center of the square. The building burned in 1887, and was replaced with this elegant building in 1889.

Much new development has taken place between Versailles and Camdenton in recent decades, but there are many fishing camps in the area that still retain the rustic character of the early days. Fishing is still the number one recreation in this area of the lake. Ernest Kellerstrass was a noted lake fisherman of the 1930s. His photo appeared on the 1936 Map and Resort Guide to Lake of the Ozarks.

This was a popular real photo lake-area postcard in the 1930s. In the 1940s, the four-photo cards became linen color with large letters. The message on the back of this postcard, mailed in 1935, reads: "Mel, this is for the whole gang, explain later. Caught all the fish we were allowed to."

This view is looking west toward Hurricane Deck from Lovers Leap as the sun sets on Lake of the Ozarks at the junction of the Niangua and Osage Rivers—in the realm of legends.

ACKNOWLEDGMENTS

This book exists because people were willing to assist me in obtaining information and photographs of people, places, and undertakings that existed largely before my time.

Without the generous cooperation of Dan Jarvis, Osage Plant Manager at Bagnell Dam, and Allen Sullivan, Superintendent of Maintenance at Bagnell Dam, Chapter One would not have been possible. They provided the Stone and Webster Engineering construction photos from the AmerenUE archives and helped me understand what those photos depicted. I am much indebted to them and to AmerenUE.

However, the photos in this book also came from other sources, including the private collections of Danny Lane of Oak Grove, Missouri; John Bradbury of Rolla, Missouri; Bruce F. James of Lake Ozark, Missouri; James E. Lawrence of Eldon, Missouri; and my own private collection.

Danny Lane's collection of "Old" Linn Creek and of Ha Ha Tonka images were invaluable in putting together Chapters Six and Eight. He has one of the best Ha Ha Tonka collections of anyone that I know.

Numerous photos in this book come from real photo postcards. The black and white photography of the 1930s, '40s, and '50s featured on the cards was superb. In most cases, the photographers remain unknown, which is unfortunate. In other cases, some photos featured on early postcards also exist as actual photos in various historic collections. Quite often, companies issued postcards using photographs produced by state agencies. Many of those photos are now in the collections of the Missouri State Archives.

I am greatly indebted to the Missouri State Archives and their knowledgeable staff. The support given by Lynn Morrow, director of the Local Records Preservation Program at the Archives, and Laura Jolley, who manages the prints and negatives, was much appreciated. The Missouri State Archives collections include the works of various talented photographers who have worked for and with state agencies throughout the 20th century. Included in these archives are photos from the Gerald Massie and Hammond and Irwin collections. Their photography was used by the Missouri State Division of Resources and Development to promote Missouri tourism during the 1940s and '50s.

John Bradbury, an historian at the University of Missouri-Rolla, provided several photos. James E. Lawrence, now retired, formerly the operator of El Rancho Resort at the junction of 54–52 south of Eldon, helped to piece together the history of that site. James Martin of Russellville contributed a Ha Ha Tonka photo, as did Van Beydler of St. Roberts, and Bruce F. James, whose late father William Bruce James was a former manager of the Osage Plant, gave me unlimited access to his father's collection of photos and dam information.

Last but not least, I am indebted to the Camden County Historical Society and Museum—Ken Parsons in particular, and the Miller County Historical Society and Museum. The photographs they provided could not have come from any other source and enriched the book immensely.

127

BIBLIOGRAPHY

Burke, Lorraine. *50th Anniversary Bagnell Dam 1931–1981*. Lake of the Ozarks Area Council of the Arts. 1981

Eldon Advertiser newspaper, Eldon. Various early issues.

Flader, Susan. *Exploring Missouri's Legacy, State Parks and Historic Sites*. University of Missouri Press, 1992

Harpham, Lucille Keller. *Camden County History*.

Hubbell, Victoria. *A Town On Two Rivers, A History of Osage Beach, Missouri*. City of Osage Beach. 1998

Jeffries, T. Victor. *Before the Dam Water*. 1989.

Lake of the Ozarks News newspaper, Lake Ozark. Various early issues.

McCanse, Keith. *Where to Go In The Ozarks*. 1932.

Miller County Autogram newspaper, Tuscumbia. Various early issues.

Missouri Red Book—1913. 35th Annual Report, Bureau of Labor Statistics, State of Missouri. 1914

Missouri's Lake of the Ozarks (map and guide). Lake of the Ozarks Association. 1936 and 1942.

Missouri, The WPA Guide to the "Show Me" State. Missouri Historical Society Press, St. Louis, 1998

Moreland, Fern. *A History of Camdenton*. Camden County Historian. Camden County Historical Society. 1977

Moulder, Nelle. *Early Days In Linn Creek*. Camden County Historian. Camden County Historical Society. 1969

Phillips, Emme. *Joseph W. McClurg*. Camden County Historian, Camden County Historical Society. 1976

Pilkington, Carole Tellman. *The Story of Bagnell Dam*. Lake Area Chamber of Commerce, 1989.

Raynor, Tina. *Eldon Missouri, A Look Back, 1882–1982*. Eldon Centennial, Inc.

Strange, Gaylord. *Dam Site, Missouri. Osage River Country, A History of the People and the Places of Miller County, Missouri*. Ketch's Printing, Jefferson City, Mo. 1995

The Arnhold Family. Camden County Historian. Camden County Historical Society. 1992.

The History of Ha Ha Tonka. Camden County Historian. Camden County Historical Society. 1985–87.

The Reveille newspaper, Camdenton. Various early issues.

Union Electric Magazine. Union Electric Light and Power Company.

Vacation in the Heart of the Ozarks. Lake of the Ozarks Association. 1939.

Versailles Leader newspaper, Versailles. Various early issues.

Visit us at
arcadiapublishing.com